Creepy Creatures

ANGLERFISH

BY TRUDY BECKER

WWW.APEXEDITIONS.COM

Copyright © 2025 by Apex Editions, Mendota Heights, MN 55120. All rights reserved. No part of this book may be reproduced or utilized in any form or by any means without written permission from the publisher.

Apex is distributed by North Star Editions:
sales@northstareditions.com | 888-417-0195

Produced for Apex by Red Line Editorial.

Photographs ©: David Shale/Nature Picture Library/Alamy, cover, 4–5, 15, 21; Doug Perrine/Alamy, 1, 7; Shutterstock Images, 6, 10–11, 12, 16–17, 18–19, 24, 29; Solvin Zankl/Mauritius Images GmbH/Alamy, 9, 27; Blue Planet Archive/Alamy, 13; Alex Mustard/Nature Picture Library/Alamy, 22–23; Solvin Zankl/Alamy, 25

Library of Congress Control Number: 2024939756

ISBN
979-8-89250-318-1 (hardcover)
979-8-89250-356-3 (paperback)
979-8-89250-430-0 (ebook pdf)
979-8-89250-394-5 (hosted ebook)

Printed in the United States of America
Mankato, MN
012025

NOTE TO PARENTS AND EDUCATORS

Apex books are designed to build literacy skills in striving readers. Exciting, high-interest content attracts and holds readers' attention. The text is carefully leveled to allow students to achieve success quickly. Additional features, such as bolded glossary words for difficult terms, help build comprehension.

TABLE OF CONTENTS

CHAPTER 1
DEEP-SEA ATTACK 4

CHAPTER 2
ALL ABOUT ANGLERS 10

CHAPTER 3
EATING AND HUNTING 16

CHAPTER 4
LIFE CYCLE 22

COMPREHENSION QUESTIONS • 28
GLOSSARY • 30
TO LEARN MORE • 31
ABOUT THE AUTHOR • 31
INDEX • 32

CHAPTER 1

DEEP-SEA ATTACK

An anglerfish floats in deep, dark water. A glowing **lure** hangs above its head. The angler is waiting for its next meal.

Many anglerfish live deep in the ocean. No sunlight reaches the water there.

Some anglers eat lanternfish. These tiny fish have large eyes.

Soon, a small fish swims by. It spots the angler's lure. The small fish is curious. It swims closer. It wants to see what the light is.

FOLLOW THE LIGHT

Several deep-sea animals use glowing lures. The lures often look like things that fish eat. An anglerfish's lure grows from its spine. It hangs above the fish's head.

Some anglers can cover their lures with a flap of skin. They use the flap to flash the light on and off.

Suddenly, the anglerfish lunges forward. Its mouth opens wide. The small fish has no time to swim away. The angler gulps it down.

FAST FACT

An angler's open mouth can create **suction**. Water and **prey** get pulled inside quickly.

An anglerfish's teeth curve inward. This helps the angler trap prey.

CHAPTER 2

ALL ABOUT ANGLERS

Anglerfish come in many shapes and sizes. There are more than 200 **species**. Most kinds are small. But some grow more than 3 feet (0.9 m) long.

Some anglerfish species have clear skin.

Some kinds of anglerfish live near the ocean's surface. Others live deeper. Waters there are dark and cold. There is not much food.

Frogfish are anglers that live near the surface. They have the quickest bites of any animal.

Most anglerfish live in the Atlantic or Antarctic Oceans.

FAST FACT

Many anglers live more than 1 mile (1.6 km) underwater.

In deep-sea species, females are bigger than males. Only females have lures. Their lures are full of **bacteria**. These bacteria make the lures glow.

STAYING HIDDEN

Some anglerfish have skin that **absorbs** light. Prey can see the angler's glowing lure, but the rest of the angler's body stays hidden. That helps the anglerfish hunt.

An anglerfish lure holds millions of tiny bacteria.

CHAPTER 3

Eating and Hunting

Anglerfish often eat shrimp, squid, and other fish. But they will eat almost anything. In fact, anglers sometimes eat dead things.

Monkfish are anglerfish that often live in warm, shallow seas. They sometimes eat water birds.

Some angler lures look like worms. Wiggling a lure makes it look alive.

An anglerfish hunts by ambushing prey. First, it waits. The angler may wave its lure back and forth. Then, when an animal comes close, the anglerfish attacks.

STAYING STILL

Anglerfish don't chase prey. Their round bodies can't swim very fast. Plus, they may go a long time without eating. By not moving much, they save energy.

Anglerfish have large mouths filled with sharp teeth. They also have large stomachs. And their bodies can stretch. That helps anglers eat lots of food at once.

FAST FACT

Anglerfish can swallow animals that are up to twice their size.

Most anglerfish have see-through teeth.

CHAPTER 4

LIFE CYCLE

Many anglerfish are solitary. They spend most of their time alone. However, they do come together to **mate**.

When frogfish mate, females may try to eat males.

In some species, a male swims behind a female. He **fertilizes** eggs after she lets them out. In other species, a male bites onto the female. He fertilizes eggs while attached to her body.

A female angler can let out hundreds of thousands of eggs at a time.

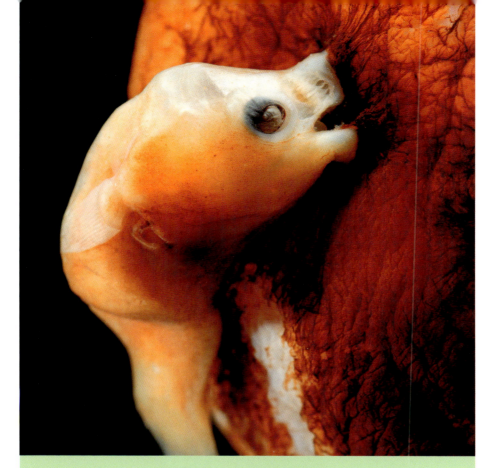

Up to six male anglers may attach to a single deep-sea female.

HANGING ON

Some male anglerfish never let go of females. The fish's bodies **fuse** together. Each male gets food from the female's blood. Often, males slowly lose their eyes and other body parts.

Baby anglers hatch near the surface. It is easier for the small fish to find food there. They may live in deeper waters as adults.

FAST FACT
Some anglerfish live up to 30 years in the wild.

At first, a young deep-sea angler doesn't have a lure. That part grows later.

COMPREHENSION QUESTIONS

Write your answers on a separate piece of paper.

1. Write a few sentences describing how anglerfish catch prey.

2. Would you be scared to see an anglerfish? Why or why not?

3. What do anglers often eat?
    - **A.** bacteria
    - **B.** lures
    - **C.** shrimp

4. What would happen if an anglerfish moved around a lot while hunting?
    - **A.** The fish would need to eat more often.
    - **B.** The fish would need to eat less often.
    - **C.** The fish would catch lots of prey.

5. What does **curious** mean in this book?

*The small fish is **curious**. It swims closer. It wants to see what the light is.*

    A. wanting to stay still
    B. wanting to learn more
    C. wanting to get away from danger

6. What does **solitary** mean in this book?

*Many anglerfish are **solitary**. They spend most of their time alone.*

    A. often away from others
    B. often close to babies
    C. often swimming

Answer key on page 32.

GLOSSARY

absorbs
Takes in.

bacteria
Tiny living things.

fertilizes
Causes an egg to start growing into a new young animal.

fuse
To join together.

lure
Something that acts as bait or draws an animal closer.

mate
To form a pair and come together to have babies.

prey
Animals that are hunted and eaten by other animals.

species
Groups of animals or plants that are similar and can breed with one another.

suction
A strong pull, often caused by removing air from a space.

TO LEARN MORE

BOOKS

Andrews, Elizabeth. *How Fish Evolved*. Minneapolis: Abdo Publishing, 2024.

Morey, Allan. *Exploring the Deep Sea*. Minneapolis: Bellwether Media, 2023.

Norton, Elisabeth. *Deepest Divers*. Mendota Heights, MN: Apex Editions, 2023.

ONLINE RESOURCES

Visit **www.apexeditions.com** to find links and resources related to this title.

ABOUT THE AUTHOR

Trudy Becker lives in Minneapolis, Minnesota. She likes exploring new places and loves anything involving books.

INDEX

A
ambushing, 19

B
bacteria, 14

E
eggs, 24

F
females, 14, 24–25

L
lures, 4, 6–7, 14, 19

M
males, 14, 24–25
mating, 22

P
prey, 8, 14, 19

S
species, 10, 14, 24
spine, 7
suction, 8

T
teeth, 20

ANSWER KEY:
1. Answers will vary; 2. Answers will vary; 3. C; 4. A; 5. B; 6. A